A GRANNIES ON SAFARI® COOKBOOK

GRANNY REGINA'S
FAVORITE
INTERNATIONAL RECIPES

Copyright © 2013, The Art Explorers, Inc.

Cover photo: Japanese fare. *Photo by M. DiDonato;* Above photo: Lomo Saltado, see page 31 for recipe. *Photo by D. Fraser.*

ISBN-13: 978-0-9792049-2-0
Printed in the United States of America.

PUBLISHED IN ASSOCIATION WITH TIGER STRIPE PUBLISHING.

FOREWORD

On December 17, 2011, my beloved culinary friend, Regina Fraser, attended my annual holiday cookie exchange. She made a platter of delicious bacon maple cookies. At that point, I knew she had a true passion for cooking creative and delicious food.

For years, Regina has traveled the world to learn about culture and cuisine from many countries. From these travels, she has decided to write this book! So, come along and take this global journey from Argentina to Zanzibar, as my friend opens up your eyes and taste buds to a new culinary venture.

WILBERT JONES

Author: *The New Soul Food Cookbook* (1996), *Mama's Tea Cakes* (1998), *Smothered Southern Foods* (2006), *Images of America: Chicago's Blues* (November 2013)
Co-Author: *Images of America: Chicago's Gold Coast* (2012)

INTRODUCTION

I love to cook and to collect recipes from all over the world. What follows are some of my favorites since we began our travel series. Some recipes I've made and others I've tasted and hope to make. As you read through the book, you will see that I have added commentary about the countries and my impressions. At the end of this book is a universal conversion chart as many of the measurements are in milliliters and grams. *Granny Regina*

Granny Regina in Antigua. *Photo by Grannies on Safari.*

TABLE OF CONTENTS

Mojito, see recipe on page 14.
Photo by Grannies on Safari.

Strukli, see recipe on page 10. *Photo by Grannies on Safari.*

Argentina

Casa Rosada or Casa de Gobierno (Government House) in Argentina.
Photo by Grannies on Safari.

*There is more to this country than the Tango, Gaucho's, and beautiful
people as the food is the star! Indigenous ingredients, Italian, African,
and lots of meat are mainstays in this country. One thing you have to
do when in Argentina is go to an Asado — or barbecue! The meat is
fantastic! But for my cookbook, I'm offering you a salad and a desert to
complete your meal. The city of Buenos Aires is a perfect place to begin
your exploration of Argentina with its fun neighborhoods and lively
night scene.*

ARGENTINE SALAD

*This Argentine adaptation of a Russian salad is extremely popular and
is found all through Argentina.*

Ingredients
- 1 cup boiled potatoes
- 1 cup boiled carrots
- 1 cup boiled sweet potatoes
- 1 cup boiled beets
- 1 cup boiled or steamed peas
- 3 tbsp mayonnaise, or to taste
- 2 tbsp olive oil
- Salt and pepper to taste

Directions

- Place oil in skillet and warm on medium heat.
- Sauté the vegetables. If you prefer, you can use a frozen mix of carrots and peas, or canned beets.
- Cut the vegetables into small same-sized cubes.
- Combine with the mayonnaise, salt and pepper to taste and serve. This is the traditional recipe. You'll find that many people do not use the beets and sweet potatoes, but try it and see how you like it!

PATAGONIAN WELSH (BLACK) CAKE

Brought to Argentina by Welsh immigrants, this tea-time cake has been incorporated into the Argentine cultural food landscape. More like a fruit cake, it's a hearty and good cake to eat.

Ingredients

- 200g/7oz raisins
- 1 tbsp honey
- 200g/7oz brown sugar
- 240ml/8 fl. oz water
- 200g/7oz of margarine
- 300g/11oz plain flour mixed
- 2 tsps baking soda
- 75g/3oz chopped nuts
- 225g/8oz crystallized fruit
- Milk to mix

Directions

- Preheat the oven to 180C, 350F.
- Butter and flour a 20cm/8-inch cake tin.
- Place the raisins, honey, sugar and water in a large saucepan, bring to the boil and boil for five minutes.
- Remove the pan from the heat and leave to cool a little then add the margarine and mix well.
- Combine the flour and baking soda and add the nuts, fruits and enough milk to make a soft mixture.
- Pour into the prepared tin and bake for 1 hour. Allow to cool before serving.

Makes 1 x 20cm/8-inch cake

Croatia

Boats in Croatia. *Photo by Grannies on Safari.*

SARMA STUFFED CABBAGE ROLLS

In this part of the world cabbage rolls are a mainstay. This recipe is from my Croatian friend Maria and makes enough for a large crowd. Maria shares her rolls with many people and they aren't shy asking when she will make them again. Here's Maria's recipe so enjoy and believe me the work is well worth the results!

Pickled cabbage (i.e. sauerkraut) dishes are a favorite especially since it is a great source of vitamins B & C during long winter seasons. Different parts of Croatia make various versions of Sarma, but this is the most traditional way. Tip. Sarma tastes the best on the second day after the juices and kraut have marinated together. *Dobar tek*! Bon Appetite!

Ingredients
- 1 cup of white rice
- 1/2 cup water
- 4-5 smoked pork ribs with bones
- 1 full head of pickled cabbage (you can buy ready to use, vacuum-packed heads)
- Brine or juice from the sauerkraut (not more than 2 cups)

Ingredients for Meat Filling
- 1 lb ground beef
- 1 lb ground pork (or veal)
- 1 yellow onion (finely chopped)
- 1 tbsp vegetable oil
- 2 tbsp of tomato puree
- 1 tsp of salt
- 1 tsp of pepper
- 1 tsp red paprika powder (or to taste)
- Vegeta© (a traditional seasoning, available in most US stores)

Ingredients for Thickening Sauce (often called roux)
- 5 g lard (or replace with vegetable oil)
- 3 g flour
- 2 g red paprika powder

Directions
- In a small saucepan, bring ½ cup of water to a boil. And rice, stir and remove from heat immediately - let it stand.
- Place 3 – 4 cups of water in a sauce pan and bring to boil.
- Blanch pork ribs in boiling water for about 5 minutes. Remove from heat and drain. Blanching softens the ribs and removes a lot the "smokiness."
- Place ground beef and pork in large mixing bowl.
- Add the Vegeta, tomato puree , red paprika, salt and pepper.

Mix all together
- In a skillet add vegetable oil and sauté the onions until they are soft and lightly golden.
- Add to the meat mixture and with your hands lightly combine.
- Add parboiled rice to the meat mixture and let sit while preparing the cabbage leaves so the flavors marry.

Prep the cabbage leaves.
- Rinse the cabbage leaves in a bowl of water to rinse off excess salt.
- Remove the head and slowly begin separating the leaves. Remove the hard cabbage core first as it eases peeling off the leaves.
- Trim some of the larger leaves that have the hard cabbage core on them (it will be easier to roll later).
- Save any ripped or damaged leaves to use later to line the cooking pot.
- Plan to use anywhere from an 8 to a 12 quart pot (always use a larger pot in case the juices boil over).
- Line the bottom of the pot with a layer of ripped or damaged cabbage leaves to prevent burning later.

Begin rolling
- Lay a cabbage leaf flat with the stem facing you.
- Scoop out a teaspoon of meat mixture and place in middle of the leaf.
- Take the wide end/core area of leaf and fold over the meat mixture first, creating a half circle fold. Meat should make about 1-2" wide oblong sausage shape inside the leaf, leaving about 1"-2" of empty leaf on all sides.
- Adjust/remove meat if the meat stretches out too much.
- Fold the right edge of the leaf towards the center and then the left edge the same – creating a small cabbage cocoon over the meat.
- Tightly roll up the cabbage, make sure the sides are tucked in. Wrap the end of the leaf around the roll to "seal it".
- Layer the broken or left over cabbage leaves into a large pot on the bottom.
- Place a layer of rolled cabbages on the bottom of the pot.
- Make sure the "seal" of your leaf is facing the bottom (this will help prevent unrolling). After your first layer is done, put 1-2 smoked ribs over the cabbage, then chop up some of the damaged cabbage leaves and sprinkle over the first layer.
- Continue this process of layering and ribs until you have run out of leaves.

Prepare the thickening sauce (optional). In a small pan, melt the lard/vegetable oil and then drop in the flour until its golden brown.
- Add paprika and stir until it begins to thicken and give a burnt/roasted smell. Add some cold water if it gets too thick - and stir. Slowly pour into your pot.
- Slowly pour any leftover sauerkraut juice into the pot.
- Slowly add more cold water until your pot is about ¾ full of liquid but do not cover the rolls with liquid.
- Take a smaller lid or ceramic plate to add weight on top of rolls – creating a little pressure so that they are compressed.
- Once the juices come to a boil, turn down the heat and let it simmer for another hour or so.
- Cook for about 2 hours on medium heat.

STRUKLI

During the winter season, it's nice to cozy up with comfort food, like this Croatian dish "Strukli," which we baked ourselves at the Regent

Esplanade Zagreb in Zagreb, Croatia. This is not a sweet dish or very savory, but a good dish to have with other dishes. I had a lot of fun making this dish with the pastry chef who I think had a lot of patience as this is a time-consuming dish to make but well worth it.

Ingredients for Dough
- 500 g (1 lb 2 oz) flour
- 1 egg
- 2 tbsp oil
- 1 tsp salt

Ingredients for Filling
- 500 g (1 lb 2 oz) cottage cheese
- 3 eggs
- 100 ml (1/2 cup) sour cream
- 1 tsp salt

Ingredients for Topping for Boiled Strukli
- 70 g (2.5 oz)butter
- 100 g (3.5 oz) bread crumbs

Ingredients for Topping for Baked Strukli
- 300 ml (1 1/2 cup) cream
- 1 egg yolk

Directions
- Combine all ingredients. Knead the dough until bubbles start to form and dough becomes smooth.
- Coat the surface with oil, cover with a clean cloth and let rest about 30 minutes.
- Combine all ingredients for the filling.
- Spread flour on a large table-cloth. Roll the dough out thin (on the table-cloth), brush with melted butter and fill with filling.
- Roll by filling the edge of the table-cloth on which the dough was rolled out. Cut into two-inch pieces. You can either boil or bake strukli. (We baked it because it comes out nice and brown.)

For the Boiled Strukli
- Place strukli in boiling water salted water and cook for 15 to 20 minutes. Once they begins to float, remove with a slotted spoon.
- Melt butter in a skillet over moderate heat; add the bread crumbs and sauté until golden. Sprinkle the strukli with the bread crumbs.

For the Baked Strukli
- Combine cream and egg yolk. Place strukli into greased casserole dish.
- Pour over topping. Bake in 175 C (350 F) oven for 30 minutes or until golden brown.

Cuba

Granny Regina and Granny Pat in a Coco taxi in Havana, Cuba. *Photo by M. DiDonato.*

POLOVORNES

I loved making these cookies for my annual cookie exchange in December. What I like most is that the cookies are crumbly and light. It's a Cuban shortbread cookie that's also made for holidays and special occasions. This is a very old recipe and in its original form was made with lard. This makes about 6 dozen.

Ingredients
- 16 tbsp (2 sticks) plus 2 tsps of unsalted butter softened
- 1/2 cup of confectioners sugar plus more for rolling
- 2 1/2 cups flour (sift before measuring, I used cake flour)
- 1/4 tsp salt
- 1 tsp vanilla (I used a little more because I like a stronger vanilla taste)

Directions
- Cream the 2 sticks of butter with the sugar until it is lemon colored.
- Beat in flour, salt, and vanilla making stiff dough. Refrigerate dough until chilled.
- Preheat the oven to 400F and grease cookie sheet with remaining butter (or use parchment paper).

- Roll dough into 1-inch balls and place them on the cookie sheet. With a spoon, press down a bit on each cookie.
- Bake for 14 minutes or until the cookies are lightly golden.
- As soon as you remove from oven, roll cookies in confectioner's sugar and set them on a wire rack.
- When they are cool, roll them in sugar again. I used the sifter, as the cookies are very fragile and if handled they make crumble.

Serve at room temperature.

ARROZ CONGRI
(CUBAN RICE AND BLACK BEANS)

Everywhere you go in the Caribbean you find dishes made with rice and black beans. Each island has a different name for this dish and a few different spices but the basic ingredients are the same. I had this dish everyday while we were in Cuba and was very happy for it to be my main entrée. The Cubans call the dish Rice Congri or "Moros y Cristianos" (Moors and Christians); this name stems from when the Moors invaded Spain in the eighth century. You can do a lot with this recipe and I encourage you to try all the versions found all over the world.

Ingredients
- 2 tsp olive oil
- 1/2 cup chopped green bell pepper, chopped
- 1/2 cup chopped red bell pepper, chopped
- Small onion, chopped
- 2 cloves garlic, minced
- 1 cup uncooked long grain rice
- 15 oz can black beans (don't drain)
- 1 1/2 cups water
- 1/2 tsp cumin
- 1 bay leaf
- Pinch oregano
- Salt and pepper for taste

Directions
- In a heavy medium sized pot, heat oil on medium heat.
- Add onions, peppers and garlic and sauté until soft, about 4-5 minutes.
- Add rice, beans, water, cumin, bay leaf, oregano and salt and pepper.
- Simmer on medium-low heat, stirring occasionally, until the rice absorbs most of the water and just barely skims the top of the rice.

- Cover, reduce heat to low, and simmer 20 minute (don't peek). Make sure you have a good seal on your cover, as the steam cooks the rice.
- After 20 minutes, shut flame off and let it sit, covered another 5 minutes (don't open the lid).

RICE WITH PORK

One of my favorite dishes and easy to make! The Cubans really know how to cook pork and in so many different ways. Enjoy!

Ingredients
- 3 lbs pork shoulder (cut up into 2-inch pieces)
- 3 cloves of garlic
- 2 cups each of water and rice
- 1 each of an onion, green pepper
- 1 can of tomato sauce
- 2 large red peppers chopped
- 1 cup of small fresh peas and small
- 1 cup of dry wine
- 1 tbsp of salt
- 1/4 tsp of pepper

Directions
- Preheat oven to 300 F.
- Ensure pork is cut into 2 inch pieces .
- Separating the fat from the meat; finely chop the fat and fry.
- Remove the "crackling" and fry garlic in fat until golden brown.
- At the same time, fry the pork meat and once it turns brown, add in the chopped onions, green peppers and the peas.
- Add water to the mixtures and bring to a boil.
- Add rice, stir and then reduce the heat to low stirring to the start to turn dry. Finish off by cooking in an oven at 300 F for 20 minutes or more and everything is cooked.

MOJITO

Granny Pat is not much of a drinker but when we were in Cuba she really loved learning the techniques for making a delicious drink; this is a Cuban standard.

Ingredients
- Ice
- 6 ounces light rum
- 12 mint sprigs, or spearmint, 8 roughly broken apart
- 6 tbsp fresh lime juice

- 4 tbsp sugar
- Club soda
- 4 slices lime

Directions
- Place ice in beverage shaker then add in the rum, 8 broken up mint sprigs, lime juice and sugar.
- Shake well and serve over ice in a high ball glass. Top off each glass with a splash of club soda.
- Garnish each with a slice of lime and a sprig of mint.

NOTES

Egypt

Egyptian hieroglyphics in Cairo, *Photo by Grannies on Safari.*

ONION BREAD

Egyptians have always loved onions and in ancient times they were considered good for fighting off the "evil eye" and illness. Sometimes it was even used as a healing poultice. Many bakeries in Egypt use chopped onions, coarse salt, sesame seeds, and grated cheese. So try this bread and maybe you will feel as if you are on the streets of Cairo!

Ingredients
- 1 large onion coarsely chopped
- 3 eggs
- 1 cup of water
- 5 cups of sifted flour
- 5 tsps baking powder
- 1 tsp salt
- 1/2 cup sesame seeds
- 1 beaten egg mixed with 2 tsps of water
- 1 tsp dry onion soup mix

Directions
- Pre-heat oven to 350F.
- Place chopped onion (all but 2 tsps) in a big mixing bowl.
- Add eggs and water to onions and blend well.

- Combine all dry ingredients and gradually add to egg/onion mix beating well between the additions of the dry ingredients.
- Form dough into a ball, and place onto a floured board and knead for three minutes.
- Roll out to ¾ inch thick and cut into large flat rounds (8" diameter).
- Brush each piece lightly with egg and sprinkle left over onion and onion soup mix on top.
- Place each on a well-greased baking sheet and bake for 25 minutes or until delicately brown.
- You can also make the bread flat or put it into a loaf pan.

CHOCOLATE CAKE

Surprise, chocolate cake is popular in Egypt! But with a twist as the spices used in this Egyptian cake are not usually found in western cakes. I had a thin slice when I was in Egypt. I was very surprised at how refreshing this cake is with a cool cinnamon frosting.

Ingredients
- 1 3/4 cups flour, sifted
- 1 tsp cinnamon
- 1/8 tsp ground cloves
- 4 ounces semisweet chocolate
- 1/2 cup brewed coffee, strong
- 1/2 cup butter
- 1 cup sugar
- 2 eggs
- 1 tsp vanilla
- 1/2 cup milk

Ingredients for Cinnamon Whipped Cream
- 2 cups heavy whipping cream
- 1/4 cup sugar
- 2 tsps vanilla
- 1/2 tsp cinnamon

Directions
- Preheat oven to 350F. Grease and line the bottom of two 8-inch cake pans with parchment paper.
- Sift together the flour, baking powder, cinnamon, and cloves; set aside.
- Combine chocolate and coffee in a small saucepan; cook over low heat until chocolate is melted, stirring constantly. Remove from heat and let cool to room temperature.

- With an electric mixer set on medium speed, cream the butter and sugar together in a mixing bowl until light and fluffy.
- Add eggs one at a time, beating well after each addition.
- Beat in the vanilla and the chocolate mixture.
- Add the dry ingredients alternating with the milk, beating well after each addition. Begin and end with flour mixture.
- Pour the batter into the prepared pans.
- Bake for 30 minutes or until cakes test done.
- Cool in pans on racks for 10 minutes, then remove from pans and cool completely on racks.
- To make the cinnamon whipped cream: Chill a large mixing bowl and beaters.
- Combine the cream, sugar, vanilla and cinnamon in the chilled bowl.
- Beat with the chilled beaters on high until soft peaks form and the mixture is thick enough to spread. Do not over beat or you will have butter instead of whipped cream.
- Assemble the cake by placing one layer of the cake on a serving plate or cake stand. Spread some of the cinnamon whipped cream and top with the second cake layer. Frost the sides and top with the remaining cinnamon whipped cream.
- Refrigerate until served.

Notes

India

Granny Pat and Granny Regina in India. *Photo by Grannies on Safari.*

INDIAN AND PEANUT CABBAGE SALAD

I made this dish while we were producing two shows on India. We were in Bangalore and this very nice lady — a friend of our hosts — showed me how to make this wonderful dish. The things I learned about Indian cooking: always heat your spices in oil first and create your own spice box! The Indian chef has a box that has small containers inside, where she keeps separate her spices. When we returned to Chicago I purchased a box and made my own spice box. The good taste comes from the layering they do of the ingredients. This is one of my favorite recipes ever!!! Also, the Asafoetida powder can be found in any Indian food store.

Ingredients
- 4 cups green or purple cabbage (finely shredded)
- 1/2 cup red onions (finely chopped)
- 1/2 cup green bell pepper (finely chopped)
- 1/2 cup raw peanuts
- 1/2 tsp ground cayenne
- 1/2 tsp salt
- 10 – 12 pieces of curry leaves (finely chopped)
- 2 tbsp cilantro (finely chopped)

- 1/4 tsp Asafoetida powder (optional)
- 1 tsp black mustard seeds
- 2 tbsp vegetable, corn, or peanut oil
- 1 tsp lemon juice (fresh squeezed is better)

Directions
- Mix the cabbage, onions, cilantro and bell pepper.
- Heat the oil and add the black mustard seeds and peanuts.
- Fry until the peanuts change color and are done.
- Take off the fire and add the curry leaves, asafoetida and cayenne.
- Pour this into the cabbage mixture. Add salt and a teaspoon of lemon juice and mix well.

Serve after 15 minutes.

MANGALOREAN CHICKEN CURRY

Ingredients
- 1 kg chicken
- 3 medium sized, finely chopped onions
- 20 cloves garlic, finely chopped
- 10 to 12 red chillies (mild)
- 7 to 8 black pepper corns
- 5-6 fenugreek seeds
- 1tbsp coriander seeds
- Tamarind, a marble sized ball
- 2 sprigs curry leaves
- 1 tsp mustard seeds
- 250 ml coconut milk -
- Coconut oil (can be substituted with any other cooking oil)

Directions
- To begin with, saute 2 chopped onions and about 12 cloves of garlic until golden brown. Add the red chillies, black pepper, fenugreek seeds, coriander seeds and continue to saute until the rest of the ingredients also turn a little brown.
- Grind all this into a fine paste along with the marble sized tamarind, creating the ground masala. Set aside.
- Saute the remaining onion and the garlic pods and after this is browned, add the ground masala and the chicken. Cook until the chicken is done.
- Add coconut milk and cook for about 2 minutes. Season with mustard and curry leaves. Serve with rice or rice pancakes or bread.

Ireland

Lavendar in Ireland. *Photo by Grannies on Safari.*

IRISH STEW

We explored a lot of Ireland and found the people to be friendly and open. One of our favorite places was a town called Ardra, which was named one of the best villages in all of Ireland. We had a good time visiting with many of the townspeople, and for lunch we went to the famous "Nancy's" restaurant and bar. They served the very best fish stew and no matter how hard I tried to pry the recipe out of them it didn't work. So I did the next best thing and got this stew recipe from someone else. I encourage you to visit Ireland and do go to Ardra!

Ingredients
- 1-1/2 lbs lamb stew meat
- 2 tsps olive oil
- 4 cups water
- 2 cups sliced and peeled potatoes
- 1 medium onion, sliced
- 1/2 cup sliced carrot
- 1/2 cup cubed turnip
- 1 tsp salt
- 1/2 tsp each dried marjoram, thyme and rosemary, crushed
- 1/8 tsp pepper
- 2 tbsp all-purpose flour
- 3 tbsp fat-free milk
- 3 tbsp minced fresh parsley

Directions
- In a Dutch oven, brown lamb in oil over medium-high heat. Add water; bring to a boil. Reduce heat; cover and simmer for 1 hour.
- Add the potatoes, onion, carrot, turnip and seasonings. Bring to a boil. Reduce heat; cover and simmer for 30 minutes or until the vegetables are tender.
- In a small bowl, combine the flour, milk and browning sauce, if desired, until smooth; stir into stew. Add parsley. Bring to a boil; cook and stir for 2 minutes or until thickened.

ORANGE MARMALADE

There's a lot of great food in Ireland and sometimes it's hard to pick just one dish to share. However, no matter where you go in the country you can find orange marmalade. This recipe is really, truly easy to make. I've added the vanilla because I had a jar in Ireland with vanilla and loved it. This is suppose to be thick so don't be alarmed, it's complete.

Ingredients
- 1 quart thinly sliced orange peel (about 6 large)
- 1 quart orange pulp, cut up (about 6 large)
- 1 cup thinly sliced lemon (about 2 medium)
- 1-1/2 quarts water
- 2 tbsp vanilla
- 5 cups sugar

Directions
- Add water to fruit and simmer 5 minutes.
- Cover and let stand 12 to 18 hours in a cool place.
- Bring to a boil; cook rapidly over medium heat until peel is tender, about 1 hour.
- Add sugar and vanilla bring slowly to a boil until sugar dissolves.
- Cook rapidly over medium heat, to jellying point, about 25 minutes.
- As mixture thickens, stir occasionally to prevent sticking.
- Pour, boiling hot, into prepared hot jars, leaving 1/4-inch head space.
- Adjust caps. Process 10 minutes in boiling water bath.

Important: How to Sterilize Jars
- Clean the jars as normal, rinse but leave the jars a little wet. Microwave for no more than one minute.
- Do NOT add cold food to hot jars, or hot food to cold jars otherwise the jar will shatter which is very dangerous.

Banoffee Pie

When we were in Ireland at the Lighthouse in Hook we were served this wonderful dessert. We raved about it and wanted to know how it was made. Our host told us that this a dessert that everyone made years ago but now is considered an ordinary dessert offering. To us it was real tasty and here it is... we loved it and you will too!

Ingredients
- 1 1/2 cups graham cracker crumbs
- 10 tablespoons butter, softened
- 2 (14-oz) cans sweetened condensed milk
- 3 large bananas
- 1 1/2 cups heavy whipping cream
- 1/3 cup confectioners' sugar
- 1 teaspoon vanilla extract

Directions
- Preheat oven to 350 degrees F.
- Mix graham cracker crumbs with softened butter and press mixture into 9-inch pie plate. Bake for 5 to 8 minutes.
- Lower the oven to 300 degrees F for the toffee filling.
- To create toffee filling, caramelize the sweetened condensed milk.
- Pour the condensed milk into a 9 by 12 by 2-inch glass baking dish.
- Cover with foil and place dish inside a larger poaching pan. Add water to poaching pan until half way up sides of baking dish.
- Bake for 1 1/2 hours.
- Once both the crust and toffee filling are cooled, spread half of the filling evenly inside crust.
- Slice the bananas and layer on top of filling.
- Pour remaining half of filling over bananas, spreading evenly.
- Whip the cream with the confectioners' sugar and vanilla and spread on top of toffee filling and bananas.

Israel

Israeli Fruit Market. *Photo by M. Dugandzic.*

ISRAELI SALAD

One of the things I liked about Israel the most is that there were so many fresh vegetable and fruit markets found on streets everywhere! This salad is really refreshing and EASY to make.

Ingredients
- 2 small cucumbers
- 1 bell pepper
- 4 radishes
- 2 green onions
- 1/4 head of lettuce (iceberg will work)
- 2 carrots
- 1 tbsp of chopped parsley
- 3 medium fresh tomatoes
- 2 tbsp olive oil
- 1 tbsp fresh squeezed lemon juice
- 1 tsp salt
- 1/4 tsp ground black pepper

Directions
- Wash and pat dry all vegetables.
- Peel cucumbers and remove the seeds.

- Remove the stem of the bell pepper and the seeds.
- Clean the onions and radishes.
- Dice into bite-sized pieces and place into a large salad bowl.
- Break the lettuce into bite-sized pieces and grate the carrots, place both into the salad bowl and add the parsley.
- Cut the tomatoes into cubes and place in the salad bowl with all the rest.
- Sprinkle the olive oil over the salad and toss to ensure the mixture is coated with the oil.
- Add the fresh squeezed lemon juice (be sure the seeds are not include), salt and pepper and toss the salad again, and serve.

RICE WITH PINE NUTS

While strolling along the boardwalk in Jaffa, Israel we came upon a group of men who were cooking lunch right beside their tourist boat that was tied up to the pier. It was break time and they seemed very comfortable laughing and cooking together right there! I moved a little closer to get a good look at what they were cooking and what did I see — a big pot with rice and pine nuts and a flat pan with great-looking chicken. I stopped and said "hello" and being friendly guys, they offered me a small plate. Not wanting to be rude, I of course took it! The chicken was moist and had a simple, but nice sauce. It was the rice that intrigued me — fluffy and filled with pine nuts. I ate it all!! All the time we were in Israel I never missed the opportunity to eat this dish. I hope you like it too and it will be one of your favorite dishes to share with your friends.

Ingredients
- 2 tbsp olive oil
- 1 cup long grain rice
- 2 cups water
- 1 1/2 tsps salt
- 1/4 tsps pepper (you can use white pepper if you prefer)
- 1/4 cup pine nuts (lightly browned)

Directions
- Heat the oil in a medium saucepan.
- Add the rice and sauté gently for 5 minutes, stirring constantly (Be sure NOT to brown the rice – you only want to be sure the oil coats the rice and in fact it would turn translucent).
- Add the water, salt and pepper and bring to a rapid boil.
- Cook for about 7 minutes on a medium high heat until the water is below the surface of the rice.
- Reduce the heat to the lowest (low) and cover the pot and cook for 25 minutes or until the rice is cooked and fluffy.
- Fluff the rice with a fork and sprinkle the pine nuts on top right before serving.

Japan

Japanese Bowl Appetizer. *Photo by M. DiDonato.*

There are so many wonderful Japanese dishes I could recommend. But for this book I have chosen two of my favorites that are easy to make — you can't make a mistake with these recipes. The Japanese take pride in not only using fresh ingredients but in how the overall dish looks when you're finished and it's presented. I hope you enjoy these dishes and think of Japan when you eat them.

STIR-FRIED CABBAGE WITH TUNA

Ingredients
- 1/2 cabbage, cut into 1 inch wide strips
- 1 small onion, or 1/2 large onion, cut into 1/2 inch wedges
- 1 can (6-7 oz) tuna, drained
- 1-2 tbsp soy sauce
- Vegetable oil for frying

Directions
- Heat vegetable oil in a large skillet and saute onion on medium-high heat until softened.
- Add cabbage and stir fry until softened.
- Add tuna and stir well with vegetables.
- Season with soy sauce to your preference.

TEMPURA

Ingredients
- 8 shrimp
- 4 ounces pumpkin
- 2 green peppers
- 1 potato
- 1 sweet potato
- Salad oil
- A little flour
- Bonito soup stock
- Soy sauce
- Sugar

Directions
- Hull, shell, and de vein the shrimp. Make a cut in the stomach side. Cut off the tip of the tail diagonally.
- Peel the potato and cut into 1/4 inch slices. Cut the unpeeled sweet potato into 1/4 inch slices.
- Slice the unpeeled pumpkin.
- Cut the green peppers in half lengthwise. Remove seeds.
- To make coating, mix the egg and cold water in a bowl. Add the flour and toss.
- Dust all the ingredients lightly with a little flour before applying the coating.
- With chopsticks, dip the potatoes and the pumpkin into the coating and twirl them around to coat them. Fill a wok over half full with salad oil and heat until 340°F.
- Drop the coated pieces into the wok and deep fry, turning them with chopsticks or tongs after several minutes. Fry another minute or two until they are soft.
- Follow the same procedure for the green pepper and shrimp, but cook for a shorter period of time until they are a light gold.
- To make the dipping sauce, mix bonito soup stock, soy sauce and sugar together in a pan and bring to a boil.

Morocco

Fez, Morocco Market. *Photo by D. Fraser.*

Morocco is an exotic country and has so many beautiful and ancient places to visit. One gets the impression that you are walking back in time when you visit Fez, and see that transportation in the old market place is as it was for centuries – by donkey. Because of the diverse ethnic and cultural influences, the food is fantastic. The mint tea recipe is a standard and everyone in Morocco drinks this fresh drink.

SPICED CARROTS

This dish is very easy to make and the results are most enjoyable.

Ingredients
- 2 tbsp pine nuts
- 1 tbsp cumin seeds
- 1/2 - 1/4 cut of olive oil
- 12 medium carrots, trimmed, peeled and cut diagonally into 1/8-inch slices
- 1/2 tbsp kosher salt
- 1 tbsp honey
- 4 tbsp fresh lemon juice
- 1 tbsp chopped cilantro
- 2 tbsp chopped mint

Directions
- Preheat oven to 350 degrees.
- Put pine nuts on small cookie sheet and toast nuts 9-10 minutes, or till golden brown; set aside.
- Put cumin seeds in heavy skillet over medium heat and toast four minutes, stirring a few times, grind cumin with mortar and pestle or spice grinder; set aside.
- Put oil in skillet large enough to hold carrots in one layer.
- Cook carrots over high heat three minutes. Lower to medium and cook two minutes longer, or till tender and golden brown. Gently shake pan for even cooking. Add salt.
- Drain carrots in colander: transfer to bowl.
- Mix honey, lemon juice, olives, cumin. Cool to room temperature and mix cilantro, mint and pine nuts.

Serves four.

Mint Tea

Ingredients
- 2 1/2 cups boiling water
- 2 tbs. Sugar
- 2 tbs. Loose Chinese gunpowder green tea or regular green tea
- 6 mint leaves, crushed

Directions
- Combine all ingredients in a medium bowl.
- Cover and steep 5 minutes.
- Strain and serve.

 Notes

Peru

Machu Picchu. *Photo by Grannies on Safari.*

PERUVIAN SALAD

This is the easiest and most tasty salad ever. Elena Rubio, my Peruvian friend can't make enough for me and my family. I can eat an entire bowl myself. Made from very few ingredients and with fresh squeezed lime juice — it's wonderful. Caution: do not use lemon juice as it does not give you the same taste!

Ingredients
- 1 large white onion sliced into thin rings
- 3 cloves of garlic (slivered)
- 2 large heads of romaine lettuce
- 2 ripe avocados
- 3- 4 limes
- 1/2 cup virgin olive oil
- Garlic salt and pepper to taste

Directions
- Slice the onions and the garlic
- Wash and pat dry the romaine lettuce and tear into pieces (I make them bigger than bite size)

- Slice the avocados into 1/2 inch strips.
- Roll the limes on the counter to loosen up the fibers, you get more juice this way, and squeeze the juice into a cup.
- Add the lettuce, onions, garlic in a bowl and gently toss.
- Add avocado.
- Pour some of the olive oil into bowl and toss making sure everything is coated, no oil should be in the bottom of the bowl.
- Add the lime juice a little at a time to control the tartness - add to your taste.
- Add salt and pepper also to taste.
- Tossing as you go until you have an equal balance between the oil and the lime.

LOMO SALTADO: PERUVIAN STIR-FRIED BEEF

Elena also told me Peru had some of the best food and more than 3,000 varieties of potatoes. When I did visit, I had to admit she did not oversell her country; it had everything she said and even more. Inca history, Machu Picchu, a thriving Afro-Peruvian community and wonderful food. Lomo Saltado and Ceviche are the national dishes, and I ate them as many times as I could! Lomo Saltado is a combination of Peruvian and Chinese cuisines and really showcases these two cultures well.

Ingredients
- 2 lbs beef tenderloin
- 2 tsps ground cumin
- Pinch of Chinese cinnamon
- 1 tsp freshly ground pepper
- Canola or vegetable oil for stir frying
- 1 tbsp minced garlic
- 1-2 Thai red chile, seeded and finely minced (for milder flavor use red Fresno chili)
- Salt
- 1 tsp red wine vinegar
- 2 medium red onions, halved lengthwise and sliced, crosswise 1/2 inch thick
- 1 1/2 lbs plum tomatoes halved, seeded and cut into sixths
- 3 Peruvian yellow hot peppers (*ajies*), seeded and finely sliced (reserve 1 for garnish)
- 6 tbsp soy sauce
- 4 tbsp freshly chopped cilantro
- 2 lb russet potatoes
- Salt
- Vegetable oil for deep frying, about 1 quart

Directions

- Peel potatoes. To prevent darkening, immerse peeled potatoes in a bowl of cold water until ready to cut. Cut potatoes into ½ inch strips. Return strips to cold water.
- Meanwhile chop all your ingredients for your beef stir-fry.
- Slice the meat into ¼ inch thick and cut into ½ inch wide strips. In a large bowl, toss the beef with pepper, cinnamon and cumin and 1 Tbs. of soy sauce.
- Heat enough oil to cover the base of a large pan or wok and , over medium heat, saute garlic and thai or fresno chile for 2 minutes. Raise the heat to high heat and working in batches, add beef strips and stir fry until browned, about 2 minutes per batch. Season with salt. Transfer the beef along with pan juice , garlic and chile to a bowl. Reserve.
- Add a little more oil to the pan or wok if necessary and stir fry onion, until barely soft, about 1 minute. Season with salt and pepper. Add a few drops of vinegar and continue stir -frying until it

has evaporated, about another minute. The onion should still have some bite. Remove onion from the pan, set aside and repeat procedure with tomato.

- Meanwhile in a heavy deep, straight-sided pot , heat oil to 375 F . To prevent splattering, pat potatoes dry. Using a spoon, carefully add potato strips, a few at a time, to hot oil. Fry for 5 to 6 minutes or till crisp and golden brown, turning once.
- Using a slotted spoon, carefully remove potatoes from hot oil. Drain on paper towels. Sprinkle with salt. Keep potatoes warm in a 300 F oven while frying remaining potatoes and continue the beef stir- fry.
- Return beef, onion and tomato to the pan. Add 2 peruvian ajies, 5 Tbs. soy sauce and cook for ½ minute. Add 2 tablespoon of the chopped cilantro and the potato fries and toss gently .Transfer to a warmed platter, garnish with the rest of the cilantro, the reserved aji and serve immediately, accompanied with white rice.

LEMON PIE

I had this pie in Lima and was told it was a traditional Peruvian pie. It looked and tasted like a key lime pie but a little sweeter. In Peru limes are called lemons so don't get confused when you are told to use lemons when in fact they use limes. This pie has a meringue top but you can omit it if you want. I like the pie both ways. Elena gave me her recipe so I could make it for Easter. Well here it is, and I plan on making one of these each year... forever!

Ingredients
- 1 1/2 - 2 cans of sweetened condensed milk
- 5 eggs (separate the yolks and the whites)
- 3/4 cup fresh squeezed lime juice
- 5 tbsp sugar
- 1 9" pastry pie crust or a graham cracker pie crust (I used the pastry crust)

Directions
- Pre-heat oven to 375 degrees.
- Put milk into medium mixing bowl.
- Add the 5 yolks and mix together.
- Slowly add the lime juice.
- For the merengue: beat egg whites with the sugar until the mixture stands up in peaks.
- Pour the milk mixture into crust, add the merengue and bake for about 15 minutes or until the merengue is brown. If you are not adding the merengue bake until the pie is dry. To test, stick a toothpick in the middle of the pie; if it pulls out dry, it's done.

 NOTES

Poland

Warsaw, Poland at night. *Photo by Grannies on Safari.*

Poland is a beautiful country and has a long history filled with culinary adventures. Each time I visit, I eat something new and different.

TANGY APPLE AND LEEK SALAD

With so many wonderful dishes from Poland, I thought this simple salad would be easy to make and refreshing.

Ingredients
- 2 apples, peeled, cored and chopped
- 2 leeks, finely chopped
- 1 tbsp lemon juice
- 1/2 cup mayonnaise
- 2 heads of Watercress or Romaine

Directions
Combine the first four ingredients and arrange on the greens.

KOTLET SCHABOWY (BREADED PORK CUTLETS)

The recipe was given to me by my friend Les and his wife, and probably because every time I go to Poland I eat this dish. Similar to the German variety, it's always good.

Ingredients
- 4 boneless center-cut pork chops or 1 lb pork tenderloin
- Salt and black pepper
- All-purpose flour
- 1 large egg beaten with 1 tsp water
- Bread crumbs or panko crumbs
- Vegetable shortening or canola oil

Directions
- If using chops, trim off fat and gristle. If using tenderloin, trim off fat, remove silver skin and cut into 4 equal pieces.
- Pound pork between two pieces of plastic wrap to 1/4-inch thickness. Season both sides with salt and pepper.
- Dredge in flour, then egg, then a bread or panko crumbs. Let the cutlets sit/dry for about 10 minutes before frying.
- Preheat oven to 200F and prepare a baking dish lined with foil. Set dish aside.
- Using a deep frying pan or a large skillet, pour oil in up to about 1 inch and turn heat on medium until hot.
- Fry one cutlet at a time cooking each side for about 5 to 7 minutes per side, until golden.
- When done, put the cutlet in the foil-lined baking dish, cover it, and place into the oven. Repeat with remaining cutlets.

NOTES

Russia

City of Kazan in Russia. *Photo by Grannies on Safari.*

POTATO LEEK SOUP

In September 2011, we were fortunate to be on the Zarengold Trans Siberian Railway from Moscow to Beijing. Our train crew was Russian and really nice. Each day we had soup for lunch and dinner, and I grew accustomed to experiencing hearty Russian soups. I interviewed the chef and he explained that he made soup from scratch and actually called his soup "whatever was available that day!" I especially liked his potato leek soup and have found this recipe that tastes pretty much like the soup we had on this adventure. And by the way.... if you want to try Russian cuisine I recommend you take the Zarengold – (http:// www.lernidee.de/en/transsiberian/trans-siberian-railway.html) - it's a 16-day trip through Siberia, Mongolia and ending up in Beijing.

Ingredients
- 3 tbsp butter
- 4 to 5 medium potatoes, peeled, and diced
- 1 lb fresh mushrooms, sliced in half
- 2 large carrots, sliced in ¼ inch rounds
- 1/2 cup chopped leeks (fresh or frozen)
- 6 cups chicken broth
- 1/4 cup all-purpose flour

- 2 tbsp olive oil
- 2 tsps chopped dill (fresh, dried or frozen) plus extra for garnish
- 1 bay leaf
- 1 tsp salt (add more at the end to taste)
- Pepper to taste

Directions
- Melt 3 tablespoons butter in a large soup pot over medium heat.
- Add the carrots and green onion and sauté 5 minutes.
- Add 6 cups chicken broth.
- Season with salt, pepper,
- 2 tsps dill and throw in the bay leaf.
- Add the chopped potatoes – cover and cook for 20 minutes. Potatoes should be firm, but tender
- Heat 2 tablespoons olive oil in a large skillet over medium high heat. Add the mushrooms and sauté for 5 to 7 minutes until they are lightly browned. Add to soup pot.
- In a separate mixing bowl, combine half-and-half and ¼ cup flour until smooth. Slowly stir into the soup and bring to a gentle boil. Soup will thicken.

If you really want it to look like Russian soup, garnish each bowl with some more chopped dill before serving.

PIROSHKI

Pies or filed pastry can be found in almost any part of the world - meat pies in Jamaica, perogies in Poland, samosas in India.

In Russia they are called Piroshki. The recipe below is fun to make and can be either fried or boiled. Experiment with the fillings as they can be savory or sweet.

Ingredients
- 2 1/2 cups flour
- 1 cup sour cream
- 1 tbsp butter
- 1 egg for brushing
- Salt to taste

Ingredients for Filling
- 4 tbsp butter
- 2 cups chopped onions
- 300 g ground beef
- 3 chopped hard boiled eggs
- Salt to taste

Directions

- Combine the flour, salt, butter and sour cream in a deep bowl. With your fingers, rub the flour and butter together.
- Wrap the ball of dough in wax paper, and chill for about 1 hour.
- On a lightly floured surface, shape the pastry into a rough rectangle 1 inch thick and roll it into a strip .
- Turn the pastry around and again roll it out lengthwise.
- Fold into thirds and roll out the packet as before. Repeat this entire process twice more, ending with the folded packet.
- Wrap it is wax paper and refrigerate for an additional hour.

Directions for Filling

- Preheat the oven to 400 F.
- Over high heat, melt the butter. Add onions and, stirring occasionally, cook over moderate heat for 8 to 10 minutes, or until they are soft and transparent but not brown.
- Stir in the beef and, mashing the meat with a fork to break up any lumps, cook briskly until no traces of pink remain.
- Mix meat-and-onion mixture. Combine the meat in a large bowl with eggs, dill, salt and pepper, mix thoroughly and taste for seasoning.
- On a lightly floured surface, roll the dough into a circle about 1/8 inch thick.
- With saucer cut out as many circles as you can. Gather the scraps into a ball and roll out again, cutting additional circles.
- Drop 2 tablespoons of filling in the center of each round and flatten the filling slightly.
- Fold one long side of the dough up over the filling, almost covering it. Fold in the two ends of the dough about 2 inch, and lastly, fold over the remaining long side of the dough.
- Place the Piroshki side by side, with the seam sides down on a buttered baking sheet.
- Bake for 30 minutes. Take them out to grease the surface with beaten egg and put back for couple of minutes until they are golden brown.
- They are ready serve.

South Africa

Fein bush in Bushmans Kloof Nature Reserve and Wellness Retreat in South Africa. *Photo by D. Fraser.*

VEGETABLE SAMOSAS

Samosas are Indian meat and vegetable pies made with a pastry on the outside and inside a filling with a variety of good things. Many cultures have something similar – England, Poland, and Jamaica, to name a few. This recipe is an example of one of my favorites.

Ingredients
- 1 large potato, peeled, diced and cooked
- 25g/1oz frozen peas, defrosted
- 25g/1oz frozen sweet corn kernels, defrosted
- 1/2 carrot, grated
- 1/2 tsp ground coriander
- 1/2 tsp ground cumin
- 1/2 tap garam masala
- 6 sheets frozen filo pastry, defrosted
- Oil for deep frying

Directions
- Place the potato, peas, sweet corn, carrot, coriander, and cumin and garam masala in a bowl and mix until well blended.
- Cut each filo sheet into half lengthways.

- Take one strip of pastry and place on the work surface in front of you lengthways.
- Fold over the bottom right hand corner diagonally so the bottom short edge is parallel to left long edge. Do not press too firmly as the crease is only to give you a guide as to where to place the filling.
- Pull the folded "triangle" part of the pastry back flat.
- Place 2-3 teaspoonful's of the filling to the left (top) of the crease guide, but not too near to the edges, and then fold the triangle part over the filling.
- Fold the triangle with the filling away from you, thus enclosing the top part of the triangle, then fold again towards the right, keeping the triangle shape.
- Continue folding the triangle in this way until you come to the end of the strip of pastry. You should end up with a perfect triangle which totally encloses the filling.
- Repeat the above process with the remaining pastry sheets. This sounds very fiddly, but by the time you've done two, you'll wonder what all the fuss was about!
- Preheat the deep fat fryer to 180C/350F.
- Fry the samosas a few at a time, until golden brown.
- Drain on kitchen paper and keep warm while you fry the remaining samosas. Serve hot.

BUSHMAN'S KLOOF ROOIBOS ICED TEA

When we arrived in South Africa and drove to Bushman's Kloof, we were tired and thirsty. Upon arrival we were handed cool, wet towels and this wonderful drink made of Rooibos Tea. The drink was so refreshing that we asked for the recipe. Please enjoy as each time we make it, we are reminded of this beautiful wilderness reserve and the wonderful staff there.

Ingredients
- 2 liters water
- 20 Roobibos tea bags (they can be found in fine tea shops and Whole Foods in the US)
- 65ml honey
- 5 star Anise
- 2 tbsp whole black peppercorns

We went to a Rooibos tea plantation and tried the tea in all kinds of food preparations. Because I like soups the recipe below is one I hope you will enjoy. And oh, the measurements are in millimeters (see the conversion chart in the back of the book for conversion).

CREAM OF CORN SOUP

Ingredients
- 1 can of sweet corn (or you can use 8oz fresh or frozen corn)
- 2 cubes of chicken stock dissolved in 600 millimeters in hot strong Roobois
- 600 millimeters of milk
- 1 medium onion chopped
- 4 black peppercorns
- 60 grams (65 millimeters) butter
- 70 grams (125 millimeters) flour
- 30 millimeters sherry
- Sour cream for garnishing
- Chopped chives for garnishing

Directions
- Simmer corn and Roobois stock over low heat for 20 minutes.
- Pour into a food processor and mix until smooth (you can run it through a sieve to make sure the mixture is smooth).
- Heat milk with the onion and black peppercorns (low heat as to not curdle the milk).
- Pour the milk through the sieve into corn mixture.
- Melt butter in saucepan, add flour and stir to make a smooth paste.
- Add the corn mixture slowly, stirring constantly.
- Bring to a boil and if the soup gets too thick add small amounts of milk.
- Add the sherry and stir.

Place in individual serving bowls and garnish with a dollop of sour cream and a sprinkling of chives.

South Korea

Kimchi jars in South Korea. *Photo by D. Fraser.*

I have been to South Korea twice and each time I find new dishes to love. The two listed below are my favorites, and I can find them in the US as well. Both are easy to make and are so tasty.

BUL-GO-GI: GRILLED MARINATED BEEF

This dish is usually served with a side of lettuce, spinach, or other leafy vegetable, which is used to wrap a slice of cooked meat, along with a dab of kimchi, and then eaten as a whole.

Ingredients
- 1 lb thinly sliced beef (sirloin or rib eye)
- 5 tbsp sugar
- 1/2 cup soy sauce
- 2 cloves finely chopped garlic (can be crushed but remove before serving)
- 1/4 tsp salt
- 5 tbsp Mirin (sweet sake, optional)
- 2 tbsp sesame oil
- 2 tbsp toasted sesame seeds
- 1 cup split green onions
- 2 cups thinly sliced carrots (optional)

Directions
- Mix all ingredients except carrots. Marinate in refrigerator for at least 2 hours.
- Cook over medium high heat until meat is just short of desired completion.
- Add carrots and cook for an additional 3 minutes.
- Serve with rice.

BIBIMBOP: BEEF & MIXED VEGETABLE RICE

Bibimbop means mixed rice or mixed meal in Korean. This is a very popular dish and can be found in Korean neighborhoods in the US too. I call it an "all-in-one" dish because you eat the meat and rice and vegetables all in one bowl. After it's done and before you serve it some people like to add a whole egg, and gochujang (red chili pepper paste). Before you eat the dish make sure you stir everything together so that it's all mixed.

Ingredients
- 1/4 lb chopped beef (ground beef is acceptable)
- 1 cup bellflower roots (doraji) (look for this root in a Korean store near you)
- 1/2 cup bean sprouts
- 1 lettuce leaf
- 3 shiitake mushrooms
- 1 sheet of vegetable jelly
- 1/3 carrot
- 1 cucumber
- 1 egg
- 3 cups short-grain rice
- 4 tbsp gochujang (red chili pepper paste)
- 1 tbsp sugar
- 1 tbsp sesame seeds
- 1 tsp sesame oil

Directions
- Wash 3 cups of rice, soak for 30 minutes and drain.
- Put the rice in a thick cooker and add 1 cup of water, then bring them to a boil.
- After 10-15 minutes boiling, reduce the heat and simmer with the lid on for 5 minutes. Do not lift the lid while cooking.
- Season beef and stir-fry lightly until cooked.
- Cut cucumbers, carrots and shitake mushrooms into match stick size and shred bellflower roots (doraji) and lettuce leaf. Squeeze

out excess water and sprinkle them with salt (not including lettuce leaf).

- Add 1 teaspoon of sesame oil to hot frying pan and stir-fry the cucumber quickly so the color stays vivid. Spread them on a big plate to cool. Add more sesame oil, then stir-fry bellflower roots, carrots, and mushrooms consecutively.
- Place cooked rice in a deep dish and add the prepared ingredients on top of the rice (*for hot stone dolsot bibimbop, heat the stone pot until hot enough to burn the fingers and coat 2 tsp of sesame oil. Place the rice sizzling right into the hot stone pot).
- Fry an egg sunny-side-up in a frying pan and place it on top of the dish (*for hot stone dolsot bibimbop, place the raw egg on the side of the hot pot so it can slightly cook).
- To make seasoned gochujang paste, combine gochujang, sugar, sesame seeds and sesame oil. Mix all ingredients well.
- Add seasoned gochujang to taste and mix it thoroughly with rice and vegetables before eating.

NOTES

Turkey

Hagia Sophia in Turkey. *Photo by D. Fraser.*

Sautéed Eggplant with Tomato-Garlic Sauce

The Turks are known for their exotic and fine foods – Turkish Delight, Turkish coffee, etc. In fact, my father who learned to cook while living overseas loved Turkish food. One of his favorite dishes was an eggplant and liver casserole. I looked for that recipe and couldn't find it but I did find this dish made with garlic that I hope you will like.

Ingredients
- 1 eggplant
- Salt to taste
- Extra virgin olive oil
- 10 oz can whole tomatoes – keep liquid
- 1 chopped tomato
- 1 tbsp tomato paste
- 2 tbsp water
- 2 tsp mashed garlic (fresh)
- 2 tsp vinegar

Directions
- Cut stem off eggplant. Remove strips of skin with a vegetable peeler.
- Cut lengthwise in half, then crosswise into 1/4 inch thick slices.
- Spread on a cookie sheet and sprinkle with lots of salt.
- Put in a colander and set aside for 4 hours. Rinse well and drain.

- Heat oil in skillet & fry eggplant slices over a high heat till they are golden brown on all sides.
- Drain. Pour off all but 1 tbsp olive oil.
- Mash tomatoes with a fork and put into skillet.
- Simmer, stirring often, 5 to 10 minutes, until they form a thin sauce.
- Blend in tomato paste and water.
- Cook for 1 minute. Stir in garlic and vinegar and remove from heat.
- Arrange eggplant slices on a serving dish and pour over sauce.
- Serve warm.

KOFTE - TURKISH MEATBALLS

Turkey was one of the most interesting places we visited in terms of history and beauty. We spent most of our time in Istanbul and would return anytime. The meatballs are wonderful and can be found everywhere - sometimes served with a spicy sauce, fresh onions. What I like about them is they can be fried, boiled or grilled. The recipe below is one I found online because it represents what we ate.

Ingredients
- 750 grams minced meat (lamb/mutton or beef, a mixture works well)
- 2 small onions, finely chopped or grated
- 2 slices of dry bread (without the crust)
- 1 egg
- Butter and olive oil to cover the bottom of the pan when cooking
- 1 bunch of parsley
- 1 teaspoon cumin
- 3 teaspoons sea salt

Directions
- Fat for cooking (we recommend butter/ghee (not margarine), mixed with olive oil). Needless to say butter helps bring out the flavor. They don't need to be deep fat fried, but do make sure there is plenty in the pan to allow the meatballs to sizzle!
- Soak the slices of bread in water, until they're properly sopping. Squeeze out excess water, and crumble the bread over the meat in a big bowl. (The bread can be omitted if you wish to avoid it).
- Then add in all the other ingredients, and knead well.
- Scoop up egg sized pieces of the mixture, and roll them in your hand to shape them into short stubby fingers. Fry on a medium heat until nicely brown.

- Serve hot with fresh bread, raw onions, salad and chilies. Rice goes down well as an accompaniment and also consider using Chili sauce or tomato ketchup. Add a tablespoon of yogurt.

NOTES

Zanzibar

Zanzibar street scene. *Photo by D. Fraser.*

FISH SOUP

Imagine you are on an island where the breeze is full of scents from spices and flowers. Where the water is clear and warm and the capital city – Stone Town – is crowded with tall white stucco walls. Spice markets are on just about every corner, and the women wear skirts infused with the scent of incense. You are in Zanzibar! Known as a spice island, it's the place to eat local fresh fish, unique vegetables, and try exotic drinks.

Ingredients

- 15 ml sesame oil
- 5 ml chili oil
- 2 shallots, peeled and finely diced
- 2 cloves garlic, peeled and crushed
- 30 ml fresh coriander stems, chopped
- 5 cm piece fresh root ginger, peeled and grated
- 1 red chili, seeded and diced
- 375 ml dry white wine
- 2 bay leaves
- 2 strips dried orange peel
- 500g crab claws
- 1kg mussels, cleaned
- 600ml water
- 2ml saffron threads
- 500g fresh fish, cubed
- 8 spring onions, washed and sliced
- 2 cherry tomatoes, peeled
- Salt and ground black pepper

Directions
- Heat the three oils in a large saucepan.
- Add the shallots, garlic, coriander stems, ginger and chili and cook until soft but not brown.
- Add the white wine, bay leaves and orange peel and bring to the boil.
- Simmer for 10 minutes and add the crab.
- Cover the pan and cook for 5 minutes. Add the mussels and cook for a further 5 minutes until the shells open. Discard any mussels which stay closed.
- Remove the mussels and crab claws and set aside.
- Strain the fluid from the pot through cheesecloth or a fine sieve and then add water and saffron.
- Bring the fish broth to a simmer and add the fish cubes.
- Cook for two minutes, then add the spring onions and cook further two minutes.
- Add the cherry tomatoes, mussels and crab claws and cook until heated through.
- Season to taste with salt and black pepper. Serve with the Pilau Rice.

PILAU RICE

When we were in Zanzibar we had this rice dish with every meal and loved it. Spicy, and wonderful.

Ingredients
- 450g/1 lb basmati rice (for a more authentic flavor and texture it is best not to use easy-cook rice; however, it will still work and be very tasty if you do)
- 1 medium onion, finely chopped
- Large knob butter, plus extra to serve
- 4 cardamom pods
- 8 cloves
- 1 cinnamon stick
- Pinch of saffron threads
- 2 bay leaves
- 600ml/1 pint hot chicken stock, vegetable stock or water salt

Directions
- To make sure you get lovely fluffy rice, wash it in several changes of cold water, then leave to soak for about 30 minutes in fresh cold water. If you don't have time for this, place in a sieve and wash under the cold tap for a minute or so.

- Cook the onion in the butter for around 5 minutes until softened. Add the spices, saffron and bay leaves and cook for a couple more minutes. The spices will give a wonderful fragrant flavor to the rice. Add the rice and stir until the grains are coated in the butter before stirring in the stock or water and salt.
- Bring to the boil and then cover with a tight-fitting lid. If the lid isn't very tight, cover the pan with aluminum foil before putting the lid on.
- Turn the heat down low and leave to cook for 10 minutes before turning off the heat. Don't remove the lid; just leave the rice to continue cooking in the pan for about five minutes until you're ready to serve.   The rice should have absorbed all the water and will just need fluffing up with a fork.
- Add a knob of butter before serving.

NOTES

Conversion Chart

One stick of butter is 1/4 pound or about 110 grams.
Butter in the US is sold in one pound boxes, each box containing 4 sticks.

DECIMALS
0.25 = 1/4
0.33 = 1/3
0.50 = 1/2
0.66 = 2/3
0.75 = 3/4

Pound, cups, tablespoon and teaspoon conversions assume the base weight-volume of water
1 pound = 2 cups
1 ounce = 2 tablespoons
1 tablespoon = 3 teaspoons = 0.5 oz = 15 grams
1 teaspoon = 0.17 oz = 5 grams
pinch is less than 1/8 teaspoon
dl = deciliter = 1/10 of a liter = 1/2 cup

WEIGHT-VOLUME OF:
Flour: 1 pound = 3 1/2 cups
Sugar: 1 pound = 2 1/4 cups

WHAT DOES IT MEAN?
c = cup
t = tsp = teaspoon
T = tbsp = tablespoon
C = Celsius
F = Fahrenheit
g = gr = gram
kg = kilogram

WEIGHT

1 ounce	30 grams	30 grams
2 "	55 "	60 "
3 "	85 "	90 "
4 "	115 "	125 "
8 "	225 "	225 "
16 "	455 "	500 " (1/2 kilogram)

Metric Conversion Chart

US	Canadian	Australian
1/4 tsp	1 mL	1 ml
1/2 tsp	2 mL	2 ml
1 tsp	5 mL	5 ml
1 Tbl	15 mL	20 ml
1/4 cup	50 mL	60 ml
1/3 cup	75 mL	80 ml
1/2 cup	125 mL	125 ml
2/3 cup	150 mL	170 ml
3/4 cup	175 mL	190 ml
1 cup	250 mL	250 ml
1 quart	1 liter	1 litre

Temperatures

Fahrenheit	Celsius
32 degrees	0 degrees
212 "	100 "
250 "	120 "
275 "	140 "
300 "	150 "
325 "	160 "
350 "	180 "
375 "	190 "
400 "	200 "
425 "	220 "
450 "	230 "
475 "	240 "
500 "	260 "

Index

SOUP AND SALADS, *continued*

VEGETABLES

Banoffee Pie (Ireland), see recipe on page 23. *Photo by B. Mayo.*